FRONT COVER

   Black Hawk, 1767-1838. This painting of Black Hawk, in full regalia, is among others by Dorothy Pate of Rock Island, Illinois on display in the Arsenal Room, Rock Island Arsenal Officer's Club on Rock Island Arsenal. The painting and map appearing in this book are reproduced by permission of Dorothy Pate, artist and cartographer. Photograph by Larry W. Wisenburg, Rock Island, Illinois.

MAP OF THE SAUK MOVEMENT TO BAD AXE

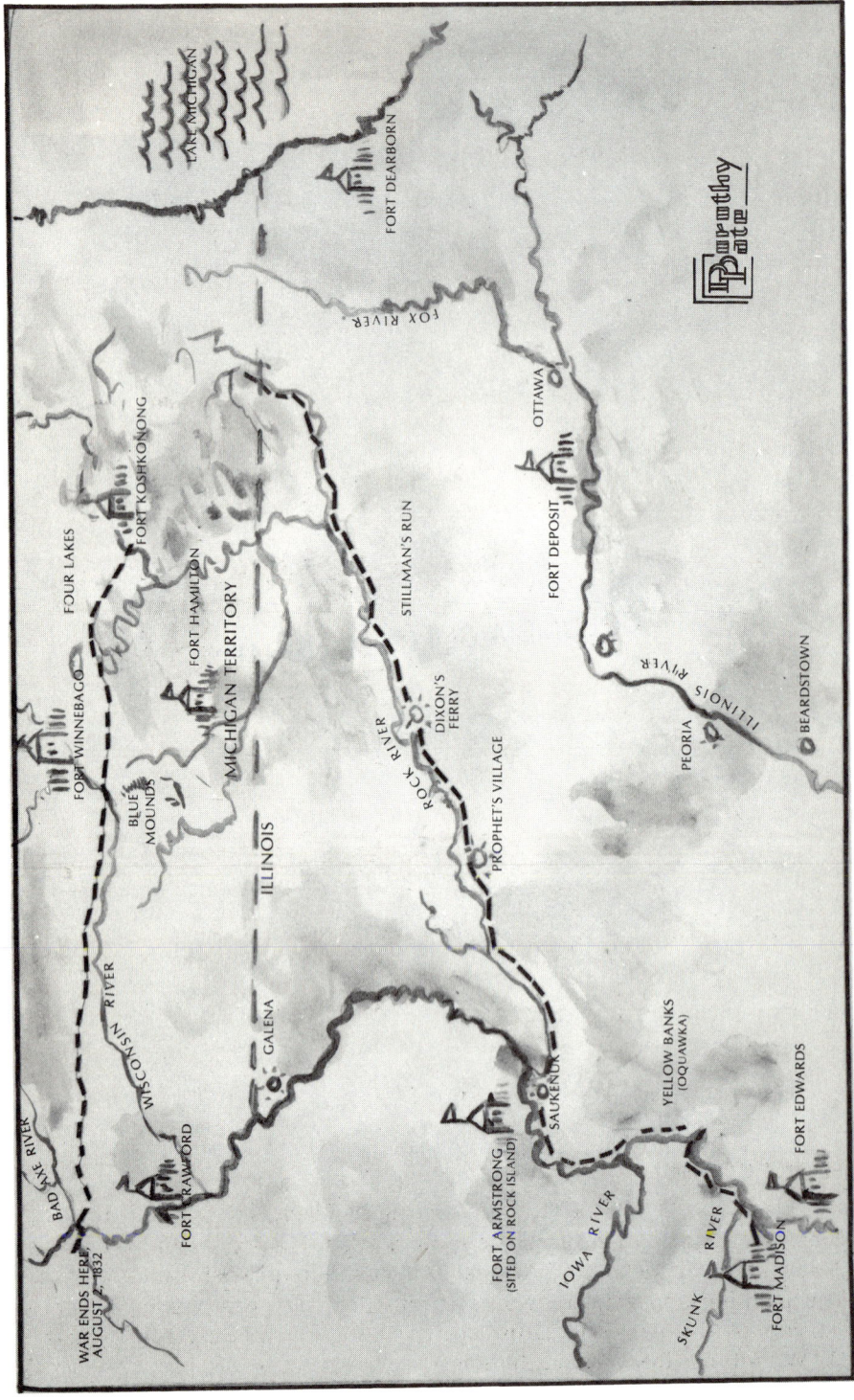

LAKE MICHIGAN

FORT DEARBORN

FOX RIVER

OTTAWA

FORT DEPOSIT

FOUR LAKES

FORT KOSHKONONG

STILLMAN'S RUN

FORT HAMILTON

MICHIGAN TERRITORY

FORT WINNEBAGO

ROCK RIVER

DIXON'S FERRY

BLUE MOUNDS

PROPHET'S VILLAGE

ILLINOIS

WISCONSIN RIVER

PEORIA

ILLINOIS RIVER

BEARDSTOWN

GALENA

BAD AXE RIVER

WAR ENDS HERE
AUGUST 2, 1832

FORT CRAWFORD

SAUKENUK

YELLOW BANKS
(OQUAWKA)

FORT EDWARDS

FORT ARMSTRONG
(SITED ON ROCK ISLAND)

IOWA RIVER

SKUNK RIVER

FORT MADISON

Parvthy
Paths

The Black Hawk War, Why?

ISBN 0-9617938-0-5

CONTENTS

ACKNOWLEDGEMENTS

Acknowledgements frequently fall into two categories, personal and technical. Technical data, obviously, must be available for the writer could not function without resource material. The bibliography lists several resources, but does not include other data also receiving careful scrutiny — all were valuable allies in the writing of this book.

I do, however, wish to thank Mr. John J. Slonaker, Chief, Historical Reference Branch, U. S. Army Military History Institute, Carlisle Barracks, Pennsylvania, for his assistance and suggestions regarding comprehensive resource material.

I certainly am indebted to Mr. Helmut M. Knies of the Hoard Historical Museum, Fort Atkinson, Wisconsin and Mr. Crawford B. Thayer, Black Hawk scholar, also of Fort Atkinson. Mr. Thayer's support also falls into the personal acknowledgement area because of his encouraging and favorable comments and suggestions. He once told me that I "was on the way to a mother lode."

The officers and membership of the Rock Island Arsenal Historical Society are publicly thanked for their support to the printing and publishing of this book.

My family should be thanked for they introduced me to a part of local history and heritage that is generally overlooked by residents near the confluence of the Rock and Mississippi Rivers. This précis could not have happened without their confidence and encouragement.

THE BLACK HAWK WAR, WHY?

* * * * * *

Lloyd H. Efflandt

Published by
Rock Island Arsenal Historical
Society, Rock Island, Illinois

From the day when the palefaces landed upon our shores, they have been robbing us of our inheritance, and slowly, but surely driving us back, back towards the setting sun, burning our villages, destroying our crops, ravishing our wives and daughters, beating our papooses with cruel sticks and murdering our people upon the most flimsy pretences and trivial causes.

These words were spoken by Black Hawk, a Sauk, as he sought support for his cause to rid his land of the ever-increasing number of white settlers. They were a prelude to " . . . that last significant Indian campaign east of the Mississippi River, inevitable climax to a two-century retreat before the uncompromising advance of civilization." This is how two eminent historians, William and Bruce Catton, describe it in their book, TWO ROADS TO SUMTER. Another historian, Cecil Eby, says it quite differently and perhaps more accurately in the title of his excellent book, THAT DISGRACEFUL AFFAIR — THE BLACK HAWK WAR.

Eby said it could have been called a bargain basement war because it didn't cost much; estimates range between three and five million dollars. Detractors of government accounting might call this a cavalier statement and the criticism could have merit. Actual costs would escalate dramatically if the collateral support, food, weapons and ammunition furnished to the Illinois civilians displaced by the war, are not included in this estimate.

Does the estimate include the cost of food and other support to friendly Indians not involved in the war? Probably not. Does it consider the cost of the land grants to the Illinois militia as additional compensation for their service? Probably not. The government may not have considered this a proper cost because the United States obtained fifteen million acres of Sauk and Fox land in the treaty of 1804 at a mere annual cost of $1000.

Abraham Lincoln might be a typical example of this windfall. Part of his service was as an officer, the last as an enlisted man. He was not involved in any fighting, yet was paid $125 and given forty acres of Iowa land and one hundred and twenty acres of land in Illinois for his less than one hundred days of service.

Other factors affected the government's prosecution of the war. The United States, hardly an arsenal of democracy in 1832, was recovering from two wars with Great Britain. Staff organization within the U.S. Army did not appear until much later. T. Harry Williams, in his book, LINCOLN AND HIS GENERALS, said that in

1

1861, the U. S. Army was operating under an "inadequate and archaic system of command;" this, nearly thirty years after the Black Hawk War, at a time when the country was fighting for its very life.

In retrospect, however, the war is a paradox, for it was essentially regional in scope. It had no major battles and lasted only seventeen weeks, yet literally thousands of words have been written about it. The estimated casualties, four to six hundred Indians and fewer than eighty whites, does not increase its stature among other American wars. In fact, Williams does not mention it in his THE HISTORY OF AMERICAN WARS.

Communication was by messenger and the U. S. Army had no cavalry in 1832. This mandated a call for mounted volunteers and, as Shakespeare wrote, "ay, there's the rub" for the Illinois militia contributed much to the ineptitude, indecision and inertia that so often characterized the operations of the Army of the Frontier.

Another critical factor adversely affecting the Illinois Indian situation was that the current U. S. president was a veteran Indian fighter. Andrew Jackson also was plagued by the irritating knowledge that Black Hawk had been a British ally in the War of 1812. 1832 was an election year and the president had to take positive steps to silence his many detractors, notably Henry Clay and John Calhoun.

A series of coincidences began in the spring of 1832 when Brigadier General Henry Atkinson, with a force of U. S. Army regulars, was ordered to Fort Armstrong in a show of strength. He was to arrest and hold for trial the Sauk warriors allegedly participating in the slaying of a number of Menominee in 1831. Black Hawk and his followers crossed the Mississippi River in early spring 1832 — neither event concerns the other.

A second facet of this coincidence is that Atkinson would not normally have been in command, but was replacing General Edmund Gaines who was on leave. The final outcome might have been different if this were not the case, for Black Hawk had known Gaines as the U. S. Army commander in the bogus war of 1831.

The United States' show of strength was intended to reduce the threat of Indian war in Illinois and Michigan Territory (now Wisconsin). The Menominee ambush, near Prairie du Chien, was the most recent in a series of incidents between the Sauk and Fox and the Sioux and Menominee. The ambush and slayings were in retaliation for the May 1830 Sioux murder of eighteen unarmed Fox en route to a meeting at Prairie du Chien. The Sauk, according to their

2

interpretation of Indian justice, considered the matter closed.

The U. S. Bureau of Indian Affairs did not see it that way, for the Sauk and Fox agent, Felix St. Vrain (later slain and mutilated in the war) demanded that the murderers surrender to the government. This zeal for one-sided justice was unacceptable to the Sauk and Fox chiefs, for no comparable demand had been made of the Sioux and Menominee after the slaying of the un-armed Fox. The Sauk and Fox leaders informed St. Vrain that the suspects would surrender of their own volition, meaning that it was unlikely that there would be any surrender.

Thus, the threat of Indian war prevailed, alarming the white settlers on the upper Mississippi. The Menominee met with the Sioux and Chippewa. The Sauk and Fox parleyed with the Potawatomi of northern Illinois while the hapless, unaligned Winnebago attempted a posture of neutrality.

Atkinson's show of strength was also to convince the Sioux and Menominee to reconsider their threats of war. Nothing in his orders indicated that the white settlements were in danger, or that the United States foresaw a war with the Sauk. Atkinson was promised additional support, if needed, from other U. S. Army posts on the Mississippi. His soldiers considered the mission troublesome, but certainly not dangerous. The ordering of Atkinson to Fort Armstrong was the first official act in what was to become known as the Black Hawk War. Atkinson received his orders on April 1, 1832 — even the calendar was against the Sauk.

A return to the summer of 1831, before the Menominee incident, will place the situation in proper perspective. A series of confrontations beginning in 1828, between the Sauk and white settlers culminated in 1831 when Black Hawk ordered the whites to vacate the land near the mouth of the Rock River.

White reaction to this was to write a letter to the Illinois governor, John Reynolds. The petition was dated April 10, 1831 and exaggerated the number of Indians in the vicinity by intimating that the Winnebago and Potawatomi were joining the Sauk. The settlers would be forced to abandon the land purchased from the United States unless the governor came to their aid. When a prompt response was not forthcoming, the whites redrafted the petition on May 15th and delivered it to Reynolds.

The governor then issued a call for five hundred volunteers, precipitating the spurious war of 1831. A force of U. S. Army regulars, under Brigadier General Edmund Gaines, was ordered to Fort Armstrong where he was soon joined by a contingent of over sixteen hundred mounted Illinois militia! This combined force attacked the Sauk village of Saukenuk at the mouth of the Rock River. This action was hardly a classic military maneuver, partly because of lack of command and control, but mainly because the Indians had successfully evacuated the village prior to the white onslaught. The army burned the deserted village.

The Sauk had crossed the Mississippi but later met with Reynolds and Gaines at Fort Armstrong. They signed, on June 30, 1831, the Articles of Agreement and Capitulation, a document drawn up by Reynolds and Gaines. The paper had the temerity to compel the British band (as Black Hawk and his followers were known) to submit to the authority of the friendly chiefs, Keokuk's party. They were to return to Iowa and not recross the Mississippi without the express permission of the Illinois governor or president of the United States. They were also forbidden to communicate with any British post or garrison. The document foisted upon the Indians had no legal authority, for Reynolds and Gaines were not authorized to enter into a treaty; therefore, the document was never ratified by the Congress. The Sauk, unfortunately, were not aware of this.

The Indian situation at the lower end of the Rock River now appeared to be settled. Black Hawk's band took no part in the subsequent Menominee massacre a few weeks later, although some of the participants sought refuge with him the following spring.

Return to the spring of 1832 and Atkinson, stationed in St. Louis, who now began to receive disquieting information from Fort Armstrong. Rumor at Rock Island was that Black Hawk planned to recross the Mississippi in violation of the 1831 Articles. Atkinson tended to discount this information and notified his superior that he would be able to neutralize this event should it actually occur. New information continued to reach Atkinson as he moved up the Mississippi. Black Hawk had, indeed, recrossed the Mississippi River with an estimated force of five hundred warriors, later reinforced by a number of Kickapoo, inveterate enemy of the white man.

Yet, part of this information was incongruous for the band not only included warriors, but also old men, women and children. Was it a war party or a migrating band of Indians? It must also be remembered that the return of Black Hawk to Illinois had absolutely nothing to do with the intertribal war Atkinson was moving north to

4

prevent.

The fall and winter of 1831 passed without incident at Rock Island because the Sauk were in Iowa. The Indian agent, St. Vrain, met with the Prophet in early 1832 to discuss the rumor of Black Hawk's return. The Prophet, half-Sauk, half-Winnebago, lived on the Rock River some thirty-five miles upstream of the Sauk village of Saukenuk. St. Vrain was told that the Prophet had invited Black Hawk to join him there. An alarmed St. Vrain promptly passed this information on to the Fort Armstrong commander, Major John Bliss.

Bliss then met with the Prophet and told him that Black Hawk's return would be in violation of the 1831 Articles. The Prophet's reply was that the Sauk were not returning to Saukenuk, but would pass peacefully near Rock Island as they moved up the Rock River to his village. Bliss warned that there would be war and urged the Prophet to use his influence to counter this. This was a hollow threat for the Fort Armstrong garrison was ill-prepared to enforce it. Desertion, drunkenness and disease were the order of the day, and the physical condition of the fort itself would not contribute towards its defense. It was with some relief, then, that the garrison and white settlers greeted Atkinson and his infantry upon their arrival in Rock Island.

Atkinson reached Rock Island before Black Hawk, but made no plans to stop him. Strengths of both sides were nearly equal, but the white infantry had greater firepower. The course of Illinois and American history might have been very different if Atkinson had taken the initative. He did not, but met instead with local authorities and Indian experts, convinced that Black Hawk's British band intended offensive action against the white settlers.

Black Hawk had crossed the Mississippi at Yellow Banks (Oquawka) but wisely avoided Saukenuk, passing near Rock Island with much singing and beating of drums. His force did include warriors, women, old men and children as reported earlier, and should have convinced Atkinson that it was a migrating movement, not one contemplating offensive action. Black Hawk was met by the Prophet and continued up the Rock River.

Since infantry cannot pursue cavalry, Atkinson envisioned a complicated campaign involving movement of the infantry by boat to Galena where they would debark and march inland against the Sauk. Atkinson, like Gaines in 1831, had no cavalry, but the Illinois militia did, and mobility had to be matched with mobility. If Gaines had been in command, he certainly would have experienced an uneasy feeling of *deja vu!*

Atkinson reported to the U. S. Army chief of staff, Major General Alexander Macomb, that the Illinois governor, John Reynolds, must again call out the Illinois militia to protect the frontier. Reynolds' subsequent call to arms, dated April 16, 1832 was successful because the gist of the proclamation was that the Indians had invaded Illinois in violation of the 1831 Articles. It exhorted the citizens that no one should remain at home while the country was being invaded and in peril. This was incredible. The only thing Black Hawk had done was peacefully recross the Mississippi River.

This second call to arms produced nearly seventeen hundred volunteers, ready and willing to lend assistance in bringing the impudent Sauk to terms. It would be inaccurate to describe the Illinois militia as cavalry. They were mounted, of course, but there the image deteriorated, for this was an undisciplined, untrained and unsoldierly force of Americans. They assembled at Beardstown to receive food, weapons and other equipage before reporting to Atkinson at Rock Island, but from this time, until the slaughter at Bad Axe, the Illinois militia would be a difficult force to control and supply.

The base pay of a private was $6.66 per month, but rose to nearly $20 if the volunteer was mounted. Other factors had to be considered — food and drink were included as were personal items such as weapons, ammunition, bedroll and camp equipment. Much of this equipment was kept by the volunteer when he was demobilized because of poor logistics control.

The volunteers moved to the Mississippi River village of Yellow Banks to rendezvous with a steamboat carrying supplies. They arrived on May 3rd but found no waiting steamboat. Many of them had discarded their Beardstown supplies because they anticipated resupply at Yellow Banks and were now forced to forage for food. This caused the local settlers to complain to Reynolds (now a Major General), comparing the militia's actions unfavorably with those of the Sauk who had passed through the area only a month earlier. This discarding of supplies later became an expensive habit of the Illinois volunteer in the field.

Two steamboats reached Yellow Banks on May 6th, one with supplies from Atkinson, the other laden with provisions from the Illinois Quartermaster General. The volunteers now received double rations and prepared to move to Rock Island. Nearly two hundred volunteers had no horses, and rode to Rock Island on the steamboats. After being sworn into federal service they were assigned to support Atkinson's infantry.

The mounted volunteers met Atkinson on May 7th, ready to pursue Black Hawk almost a month after he had entered Illinois. This delay in pursuit undoubtedly caused the Sauk to conclude that the whites intended to leave them in peace.

The militia were sworn into federal service on May 8th. This force, less the unmounted volunteers, remained under the command of Brigadier General Samuel Whiteside, a veteran of action against Black Hawk's British band in the War of 1812. The U. S. Army regular infantry and unmounted volunteers were placed under the command of Colonel Zachary Taylor, future father-in-law of Jefferson Davis and later twelfth president of the United States. Relations between the militia and regulars began badly and worsened throughout the campaign.

The force moved to the field on May 10, 1832 and the lack of leadership and discipline became evident on May 14th when two battalions of militia engaged a small force of Sauk at Old Man's Creek. The battle was promptly renamed "Stillman's Run" after one of the white commanders. Fewer than fifty Indians had routed a white force five times that number. The whites rejected initial Sauk efforts to surrender; the battle was joined and the whites suffered twelve casualties in the melee that followed. White enthusiasm for taking Sauk scalps had sustained a telling blow.

A second action, not involving the force pursuing the Sauk, became known as the "Massacre at Indian Creek." This was on May 20th with only a few Sauk participating — the main force was Potawatomi. Fifteen men, women and children of three white families were slain and mutilated. Two white girls were carried off, later to be ransomed unharmed in Wisconsin. Stillman's Run and the Indian Creek incident, as well as other Indian forays across northern Illinois created civilian panic. Conditions at Galena approached chaos as more and more civilians sought shelter there. The Sauk and Fox agent, St. Vrain, was slain on May 24th.

The civilians were not the only problem facing Atkinson for continuation of the campaign was now threatened. Enlistments were expiring and the volunteer army was foundering at Ottawa. Whiteside's attempts to stay the exodus of the volunteers failed. He later enlisted in the interim regiment as a private, and finished his service in the first battle of Kellogg's Grove.

A sobering factor affecting the continuation of the campaign was that the militia now had second thoughts about action against the Indians. It was one thing to know of death, but to see it occur violently and explicitly in the Illinois forests and plains was something vastly different. The Illinois American now had vivid and positive evidence that the Indians did not welcome the civilizing influence of the white man.

Newspaper editorials and articles decrying the situation eventually reached Washington and President Jackson, reinforcing his dissatisfaction with the progress of the campaign. Orders were issued on June 15, 1832, relieving Atkinson and replacing him with General Winfield Scott. This was a wise move, since Scott could provide needed direction and purpose to the U. S. forces opposing the Sauk. Scott was a soldier's soldier in spite of his sobriquet, "Old Fuss and Feathers."

A letter to Scott from Secretary of War Lewis Cass contained a sentence that left little doubt as to his mission: "It is very desirable that the whole country between Lake Michigan and the Mississippi, and south of the Ouisconsin, should be freed from Indians."

Scott was able to assemble one thousand regulars and supplement this by recruiting six companies of mounted rangers from the western states. This was to be a battalion size unit, authorized in lieu of cavalry, for action against the Sauk. Scott's force, moving toward the frontier on steamboats through the Great Lakes, was never an effective reinforcement since it became infected with cholera and many soliders died en route to the war.

Atkinson still needed mounted troops and would have to look elsewhere if the army could not provide them. A call again went out to Illinois for a second volunteer army to replace Whiteside's disappearing militia. The Illinois militia was the only potential mounted force available to him except Colonel Billy Hamilton's unit (he was the fifth son of Alexander Hamilton), and the newly formed rangers.

It would be unfair to report that the entire first volunteer army demobilized. Several hundred remained at Ottawa and enlisted in an interim regiment to protect the Illinois frontier for an additional twenty days. Whiteside, the erstwhile militia commander, and former Captain Abraham Lincoln, enlisted as privates in this interim force. Lincoln's participation might not have been entirely altruistic for some militiamen saw service in the campaign as excellent background to support future political ambitions. First Lieutenant Robert Anderson, Atkinson's assistant adjutant general, mustered this interim force into federal service; later surrendering Fort Sumter to a similar force of citizen-soldiers on April 4, 1861!

The second volunteer army mobilized at Fort Wilbourn, several miles downstream from Ottawa. Three brigades were formed and all officers were elected by the men. Commander of the 1st Brigade was Dr. Alexander Posey, and its strength of nearly one thousand came under federal control on June 15th. The 2nd Brigade commander was Milton K. Alexander and most of its members were from eastern Illinois counties. The unit was mustered into federal service on June 16th. The 3rd Brigade was the last to be formed but was always first in the field. Its commander was Sheriff James D. Henry, a veteran of the first volunteer army. He had also enlisted in the interim force as a private. Henry played a major role in ending the war. The muster date of this unit was June 20th.

Atkinson now had over three thousand militia and five hundred regular army infantry. Hamilton's unit and the mounted rangers under Colonel Henry Dodge were serving as Atkinson's scouts.

Latest intelligence was that the Sauk were camped near Lake Koshkonong, north of the Illinois border in Michigan Territory, now Wisconsin. Atkinson had only to lead this force north to engage a band of half-starved, hopelessly outnumbered Indians, but the Sauk had other plans. Black Hawk was not a fool, although it is doubtful that he planned any action against the whites until he knew of the second army being mobilized against him.

> With an army inferior in numbers, in cavalry, and artillery, a commander must avoid a general action. He must make up the deficiency in numbers by rapidity of his movements; want of artillery, by the nature of his movements, inferiority of cavalry, by the choice of positions. In such circumstances, the morale of the soldier is a great factor.

These were words of a Black Hawk contemporary, a monarch whose troops altered the course of European history for many years. He was Napoleon Bonaparte, emperor of France. The principles of his Maxim No. 10 were intuitively applied by an illiterate savage, permitting the Indians to successfully conduct a retrograde movement against a numerically superior, better-equipped army. Black Hawk, like Napoleon, ultimately went down to defeat but not before the Sauk had often outmaneuvered and outgeneraled the forces arrayed against him.

Black Hawk deployed several small parties from Lake Koshkonong, hoping this would cause the white commander to conclude that the Sauk were moving toward Iowa. The Indian tactics forced Atkinson to deploy over an extended area for he never could be certain where the Sauk would strike. Many of the Indians, however, remained at Koshkonong to hunt for and protect the main body of the British band.

The Indians could not fight a prolonged battle, but were forced to adopt hit and run tactics. The limited Sauk offensive involved a series of skirmishes: the battle of Pecatonica, June 16th; the first Battle of Kellogg's Grove, also on the 16th; and Apple River Fort on the 24th.

Pecatonica was a white retaliatory response against a band of Kickapoo who, on June 14th, had ambushed and slain six men working on a farm. The casualties included Samuel Wells, son of Rennah Wells of Rock Island. The senior Wells was an early settler and among those ousting Black Hawk from Saukenuk in 1831. H. L. Mencken once wrote: "Injustice is relatively easy to bear; what stings is justice." Pecatonica was the first time the whites actually stood against the Indians and with odds of only two to one in their favor. It was their finest hour!

The raid at Apple River Fort was led by Black Hawk. The fort was placed under siege while the Indians looted nearby homes, drove off livestock and left with a fresh supply of horses.

Private Samuel Whiteside was in the first Battle of Kellogg's Grove. (The former militia commander acquitted himself very well and after the battle returned to Dixon's Ferry for release and return home). The second Battle of Kellogg's Grove, June 25th, involved intense fighting. Sauk action destroyed and acquired a number of military mounts. Many of the soldier's horses were slain, others disabled and still more continued the campaign under their new Sauk owners. Eby records the thoughts of one of the soldiers as he viewed the white dead the next day: "I remember just how those men looked . . . rode up the little hill where their camp was. . . . morning sun was streaming upon them as they lay heads toward us on the ground. . . . every man had a round red spot on the top of his head about as big as a dollar, where the redskins had taken his scalp. . . . I remember that one man had buckskin breeches on." Perhaps this was a presage of things

10

to come for this soldier. He would one day know of the deaths of many, many Americans, for he was Abraham Lincoln.

The delaying tactics of the Sauk were successful for it was not until the end of June that Atkinson could regroup and continue his northward advance. Initial progress up Rock River was fairly rapid. July 1st found the army near Beloit. Scouts reported traces of recent Indian presence, so Atkinson erected breastworks in anticipation of a possible Sauk attack. The army remained in bivouac for several days, continuing the advance up both sides of the river on July 6th. The advance must continue, for the army was again running short of provisions, and it was during this time that Atkinson received word of his impending relief by Scott. He must find and destroy the Sauk without delay.

His difficulties increased; the soldiers encountered impassable terrain and the advance ground to a halt. Atkinson ordered a return to the original bivouac. The land was against the whites; Atkinson reported to Scott that the Sauk had eluded him and included a vivid description of the inhospitable terrain facing him. His woes continued when the commander of his 2nd Division, General Hugh Brady, fell ill from the drinking water and was hors de combat for the remainder of the campaign.

The army then built a base camp on the site of present-day Fort Atkinson, naming it Fort Koshkonong. Nearly a month had passed since the Fort Wilbourn mobilization and the situation was worsening daily. Atkinson ordered two of his units to Fort Winnebago to draw twelve days rations and return to the base camp without delay. The distance to Fort Winnebago was thought to be thirty-six miles — it was nearly twice that far. Fewer mouths to feed meant less supplies needed, so Atkinson took this opportunity to release large numbers of the Illinois militia, including Private Abraham Lincoln. Atkinson also requisitioned an additional thirty-day supply of rations for three thousand men from Fort Hamilton.

Generals Henry and Alexander commanded the units ordered to Fort Winnebago and were told upon their arrival that it looked as though the Sauk had established a camp near Rock Rapids, forty miles to the east. Why not, someone suggested, return to the base at Koshkonong via the Rapids and force the Sauk south or west? General Alexander opposed the plan, averring that it would be a contradiction of their orders, i.e., to draw rations and return to the base camp without delay. General Henry countered by saying that he would meet the Sauk alone if he could find fifty men to follow him! A later caucus of senior officers adopted this course of action.

The militia broke camp at Fort Winnebago on Sunday, July 15th. Alexander's brigade with members of Henry's command who opted to join him (a democratic decision) moved south to rejoin Atkinson. Henry, with several hundred hand-picked men, and Colonel Dodge's mounted rangers, rode in search of the elusive Sauk.

News of the cholera epidemic reached Atkinson on July 16th, but this information was tempered by the arrival of many provision-laden wagons from Fort Hamilton. Atkinson could no longer plead a shortage of supplies for his lack of progress. Offensive measures, however, must be practical and imaginative with a common sense approach and specifically designed to neutralize a threat. Thus far, several of these elements had been notably absent in the campaign.

Alexander's packhorses began to straggle into camp within hours of the Fort Hamilton wagons. The army was now replete with provisions, yet many of the men continued south past the camp convinced that further fighting was futile.

There was frequent communication between Atkinson and Scott during this time for Scott had permitted Atkinson to "... pursue his own plan according to his own discretion and upon his own responsibility, 'til I can join . . . him." He later commented: " . . . I cannot flatter myself that I might have done better. Nevertheless, as a new general may, for the moment, inspire more zeal and confidence, I am most anxious to make the trial."

Atkinson, without Henry and Dodge, took to the field on the 19th and followed the same route up the south bank of the Bark River that had bogged him down only a short time before. The land was virtually impassable and the army again made camp. News reached Atkinson on the 20th that the Sauk trail had been found — the Indians were breaking out of the swamp and moving west toward the Mississippi. Atkinson again returned to Koshkonong.

The Sauk, after leaving the lake area, found excellent cover and concealment, but little food. They were forced to strip edible bark from the trees and dig for wild potatoes. These proved to be fateful acts for the forage left an excellent trail for the militia. The Sauk apparently intended to move to the Wisconsin River, descend it to its confluence with the Mississippi and cross to the far shore. General Henry continued the pursuit.

The Sauk attempted no delaying tactics and took several casualties, mainly among those too ill or weak to continue. Black Hawk, keeping his mounted warriors between the whites and his women and children, fell back to the Wisconsin River where he planned to make a stand long enough to permit his people to cross the wide, but shallow river. The Indians reached the river on July 21st. Black Hawk, hearing that Henry was within a mile of contact, deployed part of his force to assist his rear guard and committed them in mid-afternoon. This was intended to be a holding action, a series of feints and ruses. It proved to be a brilliant strategy, for Henry and Dodge were unable to mount an effective countermeasure. Darkness found the militia occupying the high ground above the river.

The Sauk had achieved a tactical victory. Black Hawk had led a twenty-five mile retreat, protecting his noncombatants and enabling them to safely cross the river. He had concurrently conducted a running battle against a much larger force and ultimately slipped away at an opportune time. Sunday, July 22nd, found the river deserted of Indians and the pursuit was terminated on Monday. This action is known as the Battle of Wisconsin Heights. Casualty count is obscure. Black Hawk later asserted that he had lost six warriors; the whites refuted this by reporting at least one hundred dead!

Where was Atkinson? He had left Koshkonong on the 21st, ordering Posey's brigade to intercept the Sauk. He marched to Blue Mound where he found nine hundred militia, veterans of the Wisconsin Heights fighting. This force, supplemented by the U. S. infantry, left for the Wisconsin River on July 25, 1832. The die was irrevocably cast.

Atkinson reached the Wisconsin River on the afternoon of the 26th and spent three days building sufficient floats to support his crossing.

Black Hawk had moved downstream on the Wisconsin to the Pine River. Some Indians traveled on water, others moved inland. Plans apparently were now to move to the Bad Axe River which emptied into the Mississippi north of Prairie du Chien. The Mississippi was fordable there because of shoals and many islands. Colonel Dodge alerted the Fort Crawford commander of this possibility. A flatboat, with a force of U. S. Army regulars and an artillery six-pounder, was to anchor at the mouth of the Wisconsin to block that escape route.

The gunboat saw action on Sunday, July 29th, as several Sauk canoes tried to enter the Mississippi from the Wisconsin river. Survivors of the artillery fire escaped across the Mississippi, eluding a search by civilians, soldiers and Indians, but this was transient freedom for Hamilton and his Indians found and slew them a short time later.

More reinforcement, the steamboat Warrior, joined the preparations for the inevitable Sauk end. Its mission was to impede Sauk efforts to cross the Mississippi. The Warrior moved from Prairie du Chien to La Crosse to alert the Sioux of the Sauk intention to enter their lands. On its return to Prairie du Chien, it was met by a Sioux, on August 1st, who reported several hundred Indians at the Bad Axe River. The Warrior investigated and at 4:00 p.m. saw Indians just south of the Bad Axe. The band included Black Hawk.

The Sauk recognized the flag of the Warrior captain, a Joseph Throckmorton, and hastily made plans to surrender. The Sauk signaled for a boat to take Black Hawk to the Warrior. The signal was misunderstood — the military commander thought this was a ruse to lure him ashore. He fired into the mass of Indians, killing more than a score and wounding many others.

Atkinson reached the Mississippi on August 1st, and ordered the army to engage the Indians at 2:00 a.m. on August 2nd. An ally of the Indians was the darkness that delayed the attack because of the confusion created by lost horses. Atkinson planned to attack the main Sauk force at the river, deploying Posey and Alexander to prevent escape to the north. Henry's command was positioned to intercept the Sauk if they moved south. This was an elaborate plan against a band of half-starved Indians, especially with odds still more than four to one in Atkinson's favor.

It was the beginning of the end. The militia, encouraged by the first slaying of several Indians, broke ranks and became uncontrollable. A slaughter followed with many incidents of murder and rape. It was reported that Henry's men killed eighty-two Sauk in three-quarters of a mile, while sustaining only three white casualties.

Some Indians might have escaped across the river were it not for the Warrior. This ubiquitous craft appeared at Bad Axe at 2:00 p.m., maneuvering up and down river and between the islands, raking the Sauk with artillery fire. Other Indians attempting to escape were slain in the water.

But Black Hawk and the Prophet had disappeared.It was rumored that they had fled the previous night. Indian losses were staggering — less than one hundred reached the far shore. Only about forty prisoners, mostly women and children, survived of the more than one thousand Indians who had entered Illinois in early April.

Besides those slain at Bad Axe those Indians successfully crossing the river were hunted down and killed by the Sioux. Sixty-eight scalps were taken in a single action. The British band now ceased to be a factor in tribal politics; the way was now open for Keokuk to rule without serious opposition.

A galling fact prevented total celebration of the victory. Where were Black Hawk and the Prophet? Also, Atkinson's days as commander were numbered for Scott reached Prairie du Chien on August 7, 1832.

Survivor interrogation disclosed that Black Hawk and the Prophet had left Bad Axe after the Warrior confrontation to seek refuge among the Indians in the north. They later surrendered without a struggle and were taken to Prairie du Chien, arriving there on August 27th. They were treated with respect until their transfer to St. Louis in September. Their escort officer to St. Louis was Second Lieutenant Jefferson Davis. They were placed in irons in St. Louis where visiting hours had to be established to accommodate the many sightseers.

What was to be done with them? Scott suggested that they be transferred to Fort Monroe, Virginia, at the mouth of the Chesapeake where no guard would be required. Atkinson urged that they be escorted on an eastern tour of the United States where they would be exposed to the nation's might. They would be returned to Rock Island at the tour's conclusion.

The Indians left St. Louis in early spring, reaching Washington, D. C. on April 22nd. They met President Jackson on the 25th and moved to Fort Monroe on April 26, 1833. Six weeks later they left on a second tour that included Norfolk, Baltimore and New York. A proposal that the tour continue north to Albany, Boston and other cities was rejected — the Indians were tired and wanted to go home. They left the east on June 22, 1833, and traveled west to Illinois through the Great Lakes.

It is ironic that the Indians reached Fort Armstrong on August 2, 1833, the first anniversary of Bad Axe. Black Hawk was told that Keokuk was now the principal Sauk chief and he was to obey and respect him. This was the final blow — he had thought he was free only to discover that he had been paroled to Keokuk.

Is there an appropriate epilogue to this unpleasant phase of Illinois and American history? Should it iterate the lack of white leadership and control in the conduct of the campaign? Would it have been different if Scott had assumed command? In fairness to Atkinson, it must be concluded that Bad Axe would have happened regardless of the commander.

Should history attempt to justify the treaties perpetrated against the Indians? No purpose would be served in repeating the reasons, real or alleged, for the war and the unconscionable manner in which it was fought, or the treatment of Black Hawk after his surrender.

Why did Black Hawk decide to leave his band at Bad Axe on the eve of what he must have known would be the final battle? If he had remained, however, his mutilated body would undoubtedly have been found in or beside the Mississippi among the other Sauk dead.

White Americans, barely four years later, would experience similar defeat and humiliation in a battle where all the defenders were slain. "Remember the Alamo" became a rallying cry for vengence against the Mexicans. ("Remember the Maine" and "Remember Pearl Harbor" are other indictments against America's enemies.) Rallying cries, monuments and other memorials marking the Sauk defeat are strangely missing. Still, armies are not remembered for what they build, but what they destroy.

Sergeant Shriver wrote: "We don't know what to do with the victory." Americans in 1833 were not faced with this dilemma; their victory gained another six million acres of Indian land, at ten cents an acre, in the treaty that followed the Black Hawk War.

The words of the Roman historian, Livy, have special application here. "Vae victis" translates into a succinct "woe to the vanquished."

The Black Hawk War, why?

Bibliography

Armstrong, Perry. "The Sauks and the Black Hawk War," Springfield; H. W. Rokker, Printer, 1887.

Bartlett, John. "Familiar Quotations," Fourteenth Edition, Little, Brown and Company, Boston, Toronto, 1968.

Burnod, General. "Napoleon's Maxims of War," Translated by Lieutenant General Sir G. C. D'Aguilar. David McKay, Philadelphia, Pennsylvania, 1932.

Catton, Bruce and William. "Two Roads to Sumter," Mc-Graw-Hill Book Company, Ltd., New York, Toronto and London, 1963.

Cole, Cyrenus. "I Am A Man, The Indian Black Hawk," State Historical Society of Iowa, Iowa City, Iowa 1938.

Dallman, Lowell R. Pastor. Sermon June 27, 1982, Trinity Lutheran Church, Moline, Illinois.

Eby, Cecil. "That Disgraceful Affair — The Black Hawk War," W. W. Norton and Company, Inc., New York, New York, 1973.

Thayer, Crawford B. "Hunting a Shadow," Banta Press, 1981.

Williams, Harry T. "Lincoln and His Generals," Alfred A. Knopf, Inc., New York, New York, 1952.

"The Black Hawk War, 1831 - 1832," four volumes, edited and compiled by Ellen M. Whitney, Collections of the Illinois State Historical Library, Springfield, Illinois, 1970 - 1978.

Sources for Quoted Material

Page 1 (Armstrong 1887, 260)
Page 1 (Catton 1986, 24)
Page 2 (Williams 1952, 3)
Page 2 (Bartlett 1968, 261b)
Page 8 (Whitney 1970-78, II:592)
Page 9 (Burnod 1932, 32)
Page 10 (Bartlett 1968, 960b)
Page 10 (Eby 1973, 196)
Page 12 (Whitney 1970-78, II:831-32)
Page 16 (Dallman 1982)
Page 16 (Bartlett 1968, 125a)

This booklet is a précis of several newspaper articles written by Mr. Efflandt.

Mr. Efflandt was born and educated in Moline, Illinois. He graduated from the University of Oklahoma with a BLS degree, later earning a MS in Professional Management from the Florida Institute of Technology, Melbourne, Florida.

Mr. Efflandt served in World War II and the Korean conflict, recently retiring as a Colonel, AUS. He is a graduate of the U.S. Army Engineer School, Fort Belvoir, Virginia, the U.S. Army Command and General Staff College, Fort Leavenworth, Kansas and the U.S. Army Associate Logistics Executive Development Course, Fort Lee, Virginia.

Mr. Efflandt is married and lives in Moline, Illinois.